D0907549

When Your hope Breaks

When Your Rope Breaks
Copyright © 2009 By Zondervan

Requests for information should be addressed to:
Zondervan, *Grand Rapids, Michigan 49530*

978-0-310-31851-4

All Scripture quotations, unless otherwise indicated, are taken from the
Holy Bible; New International Version®, NIV Copyright © 1973, 1978, 1984
by International Bible Society. Used by permission of Zondervan. All rights
reserved.

All rights reserved. No part of this publication may be reproduced, stored
in a retrieval system, or transmitted in any form or by any means—electron-
ic, mechanical, photocopy, recording, or any other—except for brief quotations in printed reviews, without the prior permission of the publisher.

Interior Design By Melissa Elenbaas

Printed In China

09 10 11 12 13 · 20 19 18 17 16 15 14 13 12 11 10 9 8 7 6 5 4 3 2 1

Content in this book is excerpted from the works of three authors.

Jerry Sittser lost his wife, mother and young daughter in a tragic automobile accident. His quotes in this book are taken from *A Grace Disguised*, which he wrote three years after the accident. Sittser is a professor of religion at Whitworth College.

Joni Eareckson Tada broke her neck in a diving accident in 1967 and has now spent more than four decades as a quadriplegic. Her ministry, Joni and Friends, and her dozens of books serve as an inspiration to millions who face unusual hardship. Her quotes in this book are excerpted from two of her titles: *A Step Further* and *When God Weeps*. Some of the concepts contributed by Joni Eareckson Tada were gleaned from Dr. Dan Allender and Dr. Tremper Longman III's book entitled *The Cry of the Soul: How Our Emotions Reveal Our Deepest Questions About God* (Colorado Springs: NavPress Publishing Group, 1994).

Ruth Graham is the daughter of Ruth and Billy Graham. She experienced deep anguish when she discovered her husband was unfaithful and suffered immeasurably when she struggled through a painful divorce. Her quotes in this book are excerpted from *In Every Pew Sits a Broken Heart*.

Pain

I've wasted hours pitying myself and getting all wrapped up in imagining that my broken neck was God's way of getting even with me for my sins, when in reality he was far from being "out to get me."

Joni Eareckson Tada

Are you in a crisis of great magnitude? Cry out to God in your pain. Be honest with him about what you are feeling. Ask him to reveal himself to you.

Ruth Graham

Every week I hear stories about people's pain. I have probably always heard these stories, but until I experienced loss myself, I did not listen intently to them or let those stories penetrate the protective shell around my heart. I am more sensitive to the pain now, not as oblivious and selfish as I used to be.

Jerry Sittser

Are you suffering pain that seems unbearable? Do not fear.... faith and pain are not mutually exclusive. You can have faith and experience pain.

Ruth Graham

Paul wrote in Romans 8:26 that sometimes when overcome by suffering, we do not know how to pray. But, Paul said, our dumbness before God is not offensive to him or indicative of a lack of faith. Instead, it is an invitation for God to draw near and to intercede for us "with groans that words cannot express," like a good mother does when holding a distraught child on her lap.

Jerry Sittser

I desperately wanted to kill myself. Physically, I was little more than a corpse. I had no hope of ever walking again. How I prayed for some accident or miracle to kill me. The mental and spiritual anguish was as unbearable as the physical torture.

Joni Eareckson Tada

During his years in Nazi death camps during World War II, Viktor Frankl observed that the prisoners who exercised the power to choose how they would respond to their circumstances displayed dignity, courage, and inner vitality. They found a way to transcend their suffering. Some chose to believe in God in spite of all the evidence to the contrary.

Jerry Sittser

I have read books and heard speakers that implied that if we were really giving thanks for all things and seeing our sufferings in the light of God's Word, they wouldn't even seem like sufferings. But that sort of unrealistic, happy-go-lucky approach to trials can't be found in the Bible.

Joni Eareckson Tada

People who suffer loss feel unspeak-able pain. At times it seems almost unbearable. I have often told myself, not always convincingly, that pain is a gift, a sure sign that we are alive. Pain is a gift because it shows we have a capacity to feel, whether it is pain in the body or pain in the soul.

Jerry Sittser

I encourage you to talk to God about what you are going through. Be specific. Start by describing how you feel. Be honest about your emotions, fears, confusion, and questions.

Ruth Graham

WHEN YOUR ROPE BREAKS

Sorrow indicates that people who have suffered loss are living authentically in a world of misery, and it expresses the emotional anguish of people who feel pain for themselves or for others. Sorrow is noble and gracious. It enlarges the soul until the soul is capable of mourning and rejoicing simultaneously, of feeling the world's pain and hoping for the world's healing at the same time. However painful, sorrow is good for the soul.

Jerry Sittser

Why is my pain unending?. . .This is what the Lord says, "If you repent, I will restore you that you may serve me."

Jeremiah 15:18-19

I am in pain and distress; may your salvation, O God, protect me.

Psalm 69:29

WHEN YOUR ROPE BREAKS

Those who suffer according to God's will should commit themselves to their faithful Creator and continue to do good.

1 Peter 4:19

God is faithful; he will not let you be tempted beyond what you can bear.

1 Corinthians 10:13

Anger

"Reasons why" don't ultimately satisfy…. Those who suffer are like [the] hurting child who asks his daddy, "why?" The child opens himself up to the one and only someone who can actually *do* something about his plight. He knows his pain will be eased by his father's embrace.

Joni Eareckson Tada

I was angry at God, but I assumed that God was big enough to tolerate my anger and compassionate enough to understand. I found comfort in many of the Psalms that express anguish and anger before God. I see now that my faith was becoming an ally rather than an enemy because I could vent anger freely, even toward God, without fearing retribution.

Jerry Sittser

Do you sincerely want help or do you want attention? ... If negative motives outweigh your desire for help, ask God to change your heart.

Ruth Graham

It is natural for those who suffer catastrophic loss to feel destructive emotions like hatred, bitterness, despair, and cynicism. We must decide whether or not to allow these destructive emotions to conquer us. A bad choice will lead to the soul's death—a worse death by far than the death of a loved one or the job or one's health.

Jerry Sittser

What I would discover after [my husband's] infidelity came to light was that masking my hurts and defects—pretending I had everything together—was not the way to honor God or prove that Christianity worked.

Ruth Graham

Many Christians don't see God in their trials. If no miracles are happening … God must not be at work.

Joni Eareckson Tada

WHEN YOUR ROPE BREAKS

I felt like a beaten dog. Nowhere to turn.
No hope. Kicked again and again by this pain.

Ruth Graham

Refrain from anger and turn from wrath; do not fret—it leads only to evil.

Psalm 37:8

In your anger, do not sin...and do not give the devil a foothold.

Ephesians 4:26-27

A fool gives full vent to his anger but a wise man keeps himself under control.

Proverbs 29:11

Fear

When hardship settles in to stay, dark and brooding skepticism surges over us in a tide of doubt and fear. The only sure dike against a flood of dark feelings is "to remember." We must recall sunnier times when our confidence in God's goodness – like a piling driven deep in our soul – held strong against waves of discouragement.

Joni Eareckson Tada

By placing our suffering in the Lord's hands, we are saying, "God, I cannot fix this. I am helpless. I am totally dependent on you." This act of surrender releases God to do whatever he pleases in us, through us, and for us in our suffering. There is great freedom in letting go of our cares and letting God work.

Ruth Graham

Denial puts off what should be faced. People in denial refuse to see loss for what it is, something terrible that cannot be reversed. They dodge pain rather than confront it. But their unwillingness to face pain comes at a price. Ultimately it diminishes the capacity of their souls to grow bigger in response to pain.

Jerry Sittser

Most of the time we can manage. Like jugglers spinning plates on long sticks ... sometimes we take on more plates than we can handle and we assume that, with God's enabling, we will be able to keep them spinning. It doesn't always work that way.

Joni Eareckson Tada

Are you suffering pain that seems unbearable? Do not fear. Let your heart break if necessary. Your grief does not indicate a lack of faith on your part.

Ruth Graham

The Lord is my light and my salvation—whom shall I fear?

Psalm 27:1

Fear of man will prove to be a snare.

Proverbs 29:25

Fear no evil, for you are with me.

Psalm 23:4

Meaning

The experience of loss itself does not have to be the defining moment of our lives. Instead, the defining moment can be our response to the loss. It is not what happens *to* us that matters as much as what happens *in* us. Darkness, it is true, had invaded my soul. But then again, so did light. Both contributed to my personal transformation.

Jerry Sittser

Here is the conclusion I've come to regarding miraculous healing: God certainly can, and sometimes does, heal people in a miraculous way today. But the Bible does *not* teach that he will *always* heal those who come to him in faith. He sovereignly reserves the right to heal or not to heal as he sees fit.

Joni Eareckson Tada

Loss forces us to see the dominant role our environment plays in determining our happiness. Loss strips us of the props we rely on for our well-being. It knocks us off our feet and puts us on our backs. In the experience of loss, we come to the end of ourselves.

But in coming to the end of ourselves, we can also come to the beginning of a vital relationship with God. Our failures can lead us to grace and to a profound spiritual awakening.

Jerry Sittser

I encourage you to talk to God about what you are going through. Be specific. Start by describing how you feel. Be honest about your emotions, fears, confusion, and questions.

Ruth Graham

I don't know all the reasons why God says yes to some prayers and not others....But I ... found that God gave two conditions which must be met if our prayers are to be guaranteed answers: we must be living in close fellowship with him, and our requests must be in line with his will.

Joni Eareckson Tada

Loss makes the universe seem like a cold and unfriendly place, as if it were little more than trillions of atoms colliding together with no predictability, no design, and no reason to it. Life just happens whether good or bad. Randomness mandates that we simply live as best we can, but in the end we must realize that what happens is often arbitrary.

Jerry Sittser

God lives with us in our experience. He does not leave us alone to get by—even if we are suffering consequences we created for ourselves.

Ruth Graham

I [came] to the conclusion that one of God's purposes in increasing our trials is to sensitize us to people we never would have been able to relate to otherwise.

Joni Eareckson Tada

No one is safe, because the universe is hardly a safe place. It is often mean, unpredictable, and unjust. Loss has little to do with our notions or fairness. There is often no rhyme or reason to the misery of some and to the happiness of others.

Jerry Sittser

When we ask why, we are asserting our desire to dialogue with the God in whom we have put a measure of trust. We expect he is listening and believe he is the source of answers....asking was my way of seeking to reconcile circumstances that appeared from my limited human perspective to be inconsistent with God's love.

Ruth Graham

I realize that other people who have suffered loss have come to different conclusions from mine. Some believe that we know good and bad through the operation of natural law. Others believe that we have knowledge of good and bad through the influence of social convention. But these options seem to beg the question. Where did natural law originate? What is the source of social convention? These questions push me away from atheism and toward God.

Jerry Sittser

Timing is everything....[God] arranges for natural events to occur at specific times to further his ends. In other words, he plans coincidences.

Joni Eareckson Tada

I took the time to write down all the ways God had prepared me ahead of time for what I was … facing. This activity reinforced the truth that God was, in fact, in control of my situation. He had known what was coming, and he was faithful to get me ready for it.

Ruth Graham

Sorrow indicates that people who have suffered loss are living authentically in a world of misery, and it expresses the emotional anguish of people who feel pain for themselves or for others. Sorrow is noble and gracious. It enlarges the soul until the soul is capable of mourning and rejoicing simultaneously, of feeling the world's pain and hoping for the world's healing at the same time. However painful, sorrow is good for the soul.

Jerry Sittser

God sometimes does perform miracles. ... But miracles are not his day job, not his usual way of working.

Joni Eareckson Tada

Though outwardly we are wasting away, yet inwardly we are being renewed day by day.

2 Corinthians 4:16

It is the glory of God to conceal a matter.

Proverbs 25:2

We know that in all things God works for the good of those who love him, who have been called according to his purpose.

Romans 8:28

God disciplines us for our good that we may share in his holiness. No discipline seems pleasant at the time, but painful. Later on, however, it produces a harvest of righteousness and peace for those who have been trained by it.

Hebrews 12:10-11

Acceptance

I was forced to realize that many, many people face problems just like mine—or worse. It's a kind of scale … Every person alive fits somewhere onto a scale of suffering that ranges from little to much. The problem is we usually like to compare ourselves only with those who suffer less… when we face reality and stand beside those who suffer more, our purple-heart medals don't shine so brightly.

Joni Eareckson Tada

Though east and west seem far-thest removed on a map, they eventually meet on a globe. What therefore appears as opposites—east and west—in time come together, if we follow one of the other long enough and far enough. My sister Diane told me that the quickest way for anyone to reach the sun and the light of day is not to run west, chasing after the setting sun, but to head east, plung-ing into the darkness until one comes to sunrise.

Jerry Sittser

I decided the awkwardness of feeding myself outweighed the fleeting satisfaction of self-pity. It pushed me to pray, *Oh, God, help me with this spoon!* My secret was learning to lean on the Lord for help. Today I manage a spoon with my arm splint quite well. I didn't get back use of my arms or hands. But I did learn to be content.

Joni Eareckson Tada

If we never had to weep, we would never know what it was like to have a friend wipe tears from our eyes.

Joni Eareckson Tada

[Upon learning of an unfaithful husband] I felt like a shotgun had blasted me in the stomach, or like a fullback had knocked the wind out of me. The shock was seismic—it took my breath away. I felt flattened. Completely leveled. Then somehow I managed to recoup.

Ruth Graham

Finally, we reach the point where we begin to search for a new life, one that depends less on circumstances and more on the depth of our souls. That, in turn, opens us to new ideas and perspectives, including spiritual ones. We feel the need for something beyond ourselves, and it begins to dawn on us that reality may be more than we once thought it to be.

Jerry Sittser

My paralysis wasn't a quick jolt to get me back on spiritual track, or a jigsaw puzzle I had to hurriedly figure out. It's a long, arduous process and the hurting and hammering won't end until we become completely holy (and there's no chance of that happening this side of eternity).

Joni Eareckson Tada

If you have tried everything to be healed but nothing has changed, then has it ever really hit you that the reason you are in your present condition is that God, in his wisdom, wills it to be so?

Joni Eareckson Tada

Why me? I have asked that question often, as many people do after suffering loss. I once heard someone ask the opposite question, "Why *not* me?" It was not a fatalistic question because he is not a fatalistic person. He could no more explain why his life had turned bad than he could explain why his life had been so good up to that point. He concluded that much of life seems just to happen; it is beyond our control. "Why *not* me?" is as good a question to ask as any.

Jerry Sittser

I know what it is to be in need, and I know what it is to have plenty. I have learned the secret of being content in any and every situation, whether well fed or hungry, whether living in plenty or in want. I can do everything through him who gives me strength.

Philippians 4:12-13

Courage

Once you have expressed the hurt and frustration, you will come to a point of decision. You can choose to believe that God is either for you or against you.

Ruth Graham

I *discovered that I* had the power to choose the direction my life would head, even if the only choice open to me, at least initially, was either to run from the loss or to face it as best I could. Since I knew that darkness was inevitable and un-avoidable, I decided from that point on to walk into the darkness rather than try to outrun it, to let my experience of loss take me on a journey wherever it would lead, and to allow myself to be transformed by my suffering rather than to think I could somehow avoid it.

Jerry Sittser

Somewhere down the line I became confused and started believing that keeping my chin up—or making God look good—meant demonstrating I could be perfectly whole even in struggles, regardless of what I was truly experiencing.

Ruth Graham

What matters is the movement forward. New circumstances require new adjustments, continued growth, and constant struggle.

Jerry Sittser

Let God know what is in your heart. Tell him what you feel.... You can be real. God can handle the truth.

Ruth Graham

If we never had to face fear, we would
know nothing about courage.

Joni Eareckson Tada

Turn your situation over to God. Tell him you trust him to work it out for good. As often as necessary, renew your decision to trust him.

Ruth Graham

This matter is in your hands. . .so take courage and do it.

Ezra 10:4

Be strong and courageous. Do not be terrified; do not be discouraged, for the LORD your God will be with you wherever you go.

Joshua 1:9

Patience

The Psalms ... point us to the future, encouraging us to hold on ... for heaven is just around the corner.

Joni Eareckson Tada

Living means changing, and change requires that we love one thing before we gain something else.

Thus we lose our youth but gain adulthood. We lose the security of home but gain the independence of being on our own. We lose the freedom of single-ness but gain the intimacy of marriage. We lose a daughter but gain a son-on-law. Life is a constant succession of losses and gains. There is continuity and even security in this process. We remember the losses that lie behind us, and we look forward to the gains that lie ahead. We live suspended between the familiar past and the expected future.

Jerry Sittser

When you're suffering, life is lived in steps. Very small steps.

Joni Eareckson Tada

I tried to comfort and strengthen myself by reading Scripture, and I wrote out touchstone passages in my journal.

Ruth Graham

We simply assume, quite rightly, that daily life is lived on a continuum of past to present to future. Tasks not done today can be done next Saturday. Conflicts not resolved yesterday can be addressed tomorrow. We really *must* live that way. It is impossible to pack into one day all the living that we want to do over a lifetime. Careers, relationships, and experiences unfold only gradually over time.

Jerry Sittser

Suffering has done a job on my character. Not so sloppy about relationships. Stick to promises. Am more patient, at least somewhat. People matter more.

Joni Eareckson Tada

Be strong and take heart and wait for the Lord.

Psalm 27:14

God has said, "Never will I leave you; never will I forsake you."

Hebrews 13:5

We rejoice in our sufferings because we know that suffering produces perseverance; perseverance, character; and character, hope.

Romans 5:3-4

Hope

Regret causes us to repeat a litany of "if onlys": "if only I had tried harder to make the marriage work. . .,," "If only I had gone to the doctor sooner, when I first noticed the symptoms. . .," "If only I had not spoken in such anger. . . ."

Regret keeps the wounds of loss from healing, putting us in a perpetual state of guilt.

If I want transformation I must let go of my regrets over what could have been and pursue what can be.

Jerry Sittser

He hates all the pain and heartache that come with suffering, but he has in mind a grand and more glorious end. God permits what he hates to accomplish that which he loves.

Joni Eareckson Tada

Are you trying to deal with a crisis by yourself? While we must exercise wisdom when it comes to sharing our personal issues, we were not made to carry burdens alone. Yes, we have the Lord, but he gave us people....We need trusted friends and loved ones to help us shoulder the load.

Ruth Graham

My brother-in-law wisely observed that if I really wanted to protect myself from accidents I should lock myself inside an antiseptic bubble and live there for the rest of my life. But who would want that? Better to brace myself for accidents and endure them as best I can. Better to give up my quest for control and live in hope. Maybe that is why most people seem to weather loss so well. They learn to live in hope.

Jerry Sittser

Being paralyzed has really made heaven come alive. Not in a cop-out way, but in a way that makes me want to live better here because more is coming there.

Joni Eareckson Tada

Eventually, I discovered I was not the only one in church whose life had taken unwelcome turns. I was not the only one who had missed opportunities. I was not the only one who had sinned. In particular, I found that when others were honest with me about their faults and imperfections, I became more comfortable sharing my own mistakes.... That is when real ministry and healing take place.

Ruth Graham

I have often imagined my story fitting into some greater scheme, the half of which I may never fathom. I simply do not see the bigger picture, but I choose to believe that there is a bigger picture and that my loss is part of some wonderful story authored by God himself.

Jerry Sittser

Because everyone knows something about problems and pain, we can be certain the Bible is speaking to all of us when it speaks about suffering, no matter how much or how little we have had to endure.

Joni Eareckson Tada

Find rest, O my soul, in God alone; my hope comes from him.

Psalm 62:5

Jesus said, "With God all things are possible."
Matthew 19:26

Hope that is seen is not hope at all. Who hopes for what he already has? But if we hope for what we do not yet have, we wait for it patiently.

Romans 8:24-25

Though [God] slay me, yet will I hope in him. . .In-deed, this will turn out for my deliverance.

Job 13:15-16

I consider that our present sufferings are not worth comparing with the glory that will be revealed in us.

Romans 8:18

Portions of the text in this title were excerpted from *A Step Further* and *When God Weeps* by Joni Eareckson Tada and Steve Estes which are available at your local bookstore.

978-0-310-23971-0   978-0-310-23835-5

Text from Ruth Graham was excerpted from *In Every Pew Sits a Broken Heart* which is available at your local bookstore.

Text from Jerry Sittser was excerpted from *A Grace Disguised* which is available at your local bookstore.

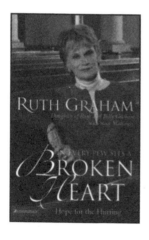

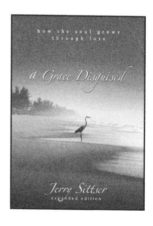

 978-0-310-24339-7

978-0-310-25895-7